Learning about God

Written
and Illustrated by
Susan Weems Taylor

Outskirts Press, Inc.
http://www.outskirtspress.com

Paperback ISBN: 978-1-9772-3742-2
Hardback ISBN: 978-1-9772-4055-2

Dedication:

To Jessica and to Adam,

To Isla and to Olivia,

and to all grandchildren

everywhere, no matter your age.

Design and layout by Kym Bloom

Note to the adult reader:

Please, as you read this book to your child or discuss it with your young reader, keep in mind that it is a personal reflection of faith. Looking for a book similar to this for my grandchildren, I decided to write one. Scriptural references are usually two or three out of many that could have been chosen. If I left out verses you feel important, please find them and share them with your child. If you are unfamiliar with the Bible, these suggested passages might be a good place to start acquainting yourself with God's message to mankind — His love letter.

If you do not have a Bible, many downloads are available. Biblegateway.com is online with probably every translation and dozens of languages. After typing in the verse, up to five translations can be placed parallel on your screen and studied simultaneously. It is a wonderful resource and reference. And there are others!

When later in the text there is reference to God's surprises and their revelation and discovery, please think of our own time and how we learn of things smaller than could be believed (the electron microscope), larger than ever dreamed (space travel and the Hubble), genetics, medicine, archeology, anthropology, the computer/digital age — on and on. Given brains, curiosity, creativity and many other gifts by the Lord, how exhilarating it is to explore, discover, and invent as we use those gifts — hopefully for the greater good of humanity.

As you move into the creationist part of the text, please know that I am not a scientist nor do I think God intended the Bible to be a static science textbook. However, the amazing sequencing of the origin of the universe in those few short verses in Genesis I find wondrous indeed. In God's family, there are many who fervently believe the cosmos was created in six 24-hour days as we count time today. Certainly in Scripture, a day has that meaning in most instances. When we are told that "unto you is born this day in the city of David a Savior that is Christ the Lord," no one questions that "day" means this literal day. But certainly the use of "day" has also been used in Scripture to denote an undetermined length of time. The book of Isaiah makes reference to "the day of the Lord" repeatedly and that is a day of how long? As long as the Lord needs it to be, wants it to be.

In II Peter 3:8, the Apostle Paul reminds us: "With the Lord a day is like a thousand years, and a thousand years are like a day." With that admonition I feel we must remember that God, the Ancient of Days, is outside of time — always — as we who are mortal know it.

I Timothy 1:17
Revelation 1:8

Let me tell you about this wonderful being. He is alive this very minute. He is the king of all things. He cannot be seen except in the beauty of his creation. But those who know Him feel the wonder of His presence.

His name is God. The amazing thing about God is that He did not come from anywhere. He just WAS and IS and always WILL BE forever. The Bible calls Him "the everlasting God".

What is the Bible?
The Bible is the most special book ever written.

Long ago and at different times many writers were inspired by God to write the Bible so that God could tell us about Himself, and how He loves us and how He hopes that we will love Him and obey Him, for He knows everything and has perfect wisdom.

It is so sweet to think how much God hopes that we will love Him, and choose to hold Him near throughout our lives.

2 Timothy 3:16
Psalm 116:1-2

But God began creating His universe long before He made people. Before God began His great work there was only darkness. And in that darkness was only nothing.

Now to think how that must have been, just close your eyes. Now put your hands over your eyes. That is how dark it was and there was nothing else. Only dark, dark, dark…

But God the super inventor, designer, artist was planning a dazzling creation. The first book of our Bible, a book called Genesis, tells this wonderful and exciting story. Let's read about it!

Genesis 1:2

The Bible says,
"In the beginning God created
the heavens and the earth".

Well, that is a short little sentence about a lot going on!

BANG! It happened very fast!
It was the beginning of everything,
even time as we know it!
We guess that from a tiny spark of pure power space
exploded, everything was burning hot,
all kinds of forces and energy started going wild,
the atmosphere was thick with
all kinds of matter, particles and dust,
and everything started
getting bigger and bigger and bigger and
GOD spoke the universe into existence...

Genesis 1: 1-3

And now the Bible tells us that the planet earth we live on had been created, but it had no form and everything was still very dark. And wet!

But the Bible says that the Spirit of God was moving over the water and so we know He was controlling and planning what would happen next.

Darkness, darkness—perhaps thick dust and cosmic particles were still swirling around the earth,
but when God commanded light then particles began to drift and settle.

However it happened we know this:

"And God said, 'Let there be light' and there was light."

Genesis 1: 1-3

And then God separated the light from darkness.
He gave us the dark and restful time He called
"night"
and the bright, light time He called
"day".
God gave us both night and day
for very special reasons, for
He was preparing our earth,
the planet we live on, for life.

"And there was evening and
there was morning,
one day."

Genesis 1: 4-5

And now God pulled the sky out of the heavy mist
and vapor up above and the waters down below.
And when the vault of heaven and the atmosphere were finished,
just like God knew they had to be to protect and refresh the earth
and all He would put there,
He was finished with the second day.

Genesis 1: 6-8
Hebrews 1:10

Now let's talk about these "days" we read about as God was creating His universe.

Some people who love God and love the Bible think each day of creation meant from the morning to the night, a day just like we know it. Six days.

But there are also many people who love God and love the Bible who think each "day" meant a very long period of time and that God chose to use this time (millions and billions of years) to experiment while carrying out His marvelous plan. It was His universe and maybe He felt there was no need to hurry!

Deuteronomy 29:29
Isaiah 45:11

And there are
some people who think
everything just happened—
somehow—somewhere—sometime—
and without God or any sort of plan—
sort of like vegetables and sausages
and noodles whirling out the air
by themselves into a handy pot of water
and becoming soup—magic soup!!
Can you believe it?
Magic universe!!
Can you believe it?

1 Corinthians 2:7
Colossians 2: 2-4

Yet it seems
that most people who
love God and love the Bible
believe that no one
can really understand
this beginning of all things,
so they learn what they can,
delight in God's mystery,
cherish His love,
and believe He will
slowly reveal His surprises when
He wants us to know them, just
as He has always done.

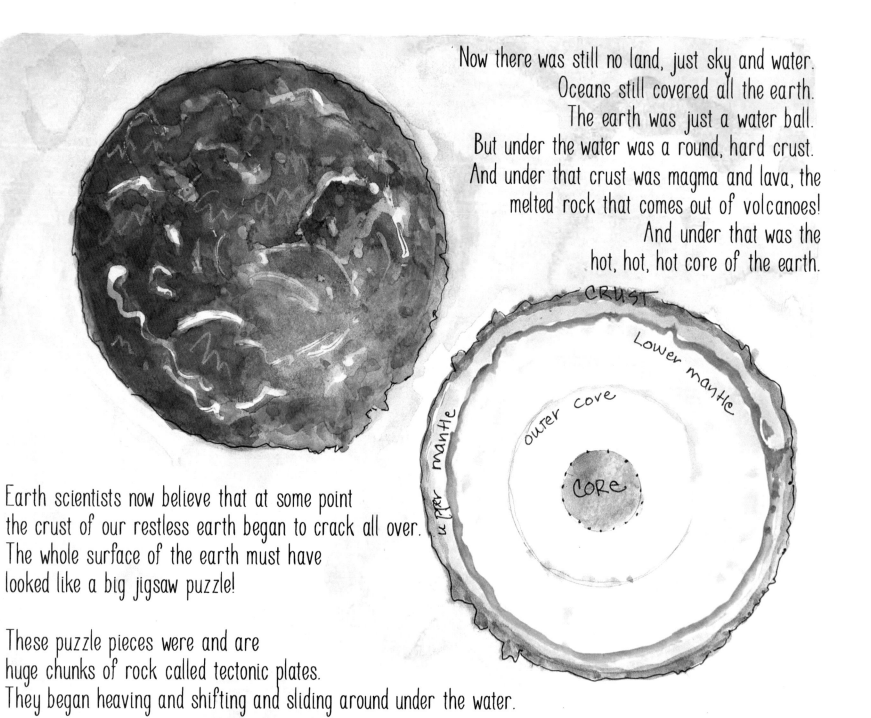

Now there was still no land, just sky and water.
Oceans still covered all the earth.
The earth was just a water ball.
But under the water was a round, hard crust.
And under that crust was magma and lava, the
melted rock that comes out of volcanoes!
And under that was the
hot, hot, hot core of the earth.

CRUST

Lower mantle

outer core

upper mantle

CORE

Earth scientists now believe that at some point
the crust of our restless earth began to crack all over.
The whole surface of the earth must have
looked like a big jigsaw puzzle!

These puzzle pieces were and are
huge chunks of rock called tectonic plates.
They began heaving and shifting and sliding around under the water.

Volcanoes pushed up mountains and made islands
as the cracks in the earth's crust allowed the boiling lava deep in the
earth to find a place to burst out.
Sometimes small islands would drift and stick together
to make larger pieces of land.
Constantly changing, moving, drifting
some plates pushed up above the water that covered the earth,
and some slowly, slowly settled into the ocean floor.

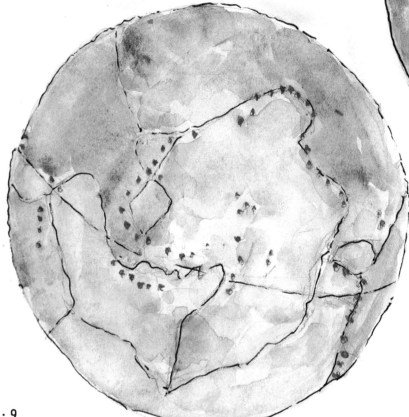

"And God said, 'Let the waters under the
Heavens be gathered into one place, and
let the dry land appear.'"

And that's what happened!

Genesis 1: 9
Psalm 24: 1-2

So now there was dry land and dirt to grow plants and plants of all kinds began to appear. Think about all the plants we have today: plants for beauty, plants for food! Plants for medicine, plants for building, plants for clothes! We have plants for the desert, plants for the mountains, plants for the prairies, plants for the jungles, and plants for the oceans, lakes and rivers. Huge plants, tiny plants! Can you imagine the world without them?

We could not survive!

And God, who provides so well for us, had the clever idea to put seeds in plants so they could always keep growing–either in the wild by themselves or so that later we could learn to plant them where we want and need them. And God designed plants so they would give us fresh oxygen to breathe, and help keep our planet clean.

Genesis 1: 11-13

Have you ever planted a garden? Isn't it a miracle that you can plant a tiny seed and sometime later have a big pumpkin, zinnias blazing with color and a morning glory up to your roof? Remember to praise and thank God for His beautiful ideas!

"And God saw that it was good. And there was evening and there was morning, a third day."

Genesis 1: 14-19
Psalms 136: 7-9

On the fourth day God decided where to place two very great and fabulous lights.
Can you guess what they are?

He set into the heavens the beautiful moon to gleam and glow in the darkness of night, and the sun, strong and burning hot, to warm us, to make plants grow, and to light our day.

Genesis 1: 14
Psalm 104:19-23

Once again God had another wonderful idea—He decided to make the sun and moon work in perfect order,
to give us a way to mark the hours and days and years and seasons. And we still use that!
Our clocks and our calendars are still based on these very things!

Genesis 1: 16-19
Psalm 8:3,4
Psalm 147:4
Isaiah 40:26
Jeremiah 31:35

And then God thought of something so incredibly beautiful and gave us another astonishing gift. He threw the stars into the Heavens and they go on and on and on— millions, billions, trillions, zillions, and no one knows how far they go!

They flash and shine and twinkle, those jewels of the night, and delight us with their beauty and mystery.

"And there was evening and there was morning, a fourth day."

Genesis 1: 20, 21

And now during this next period of creation God decided to put living things into the ocean, and living things into the sky. Because of God's command the oceans teem with life of all kinds—from the tiniest little animals that can only be seen under a microscope to huge blue whales—the largest creatures now on earth!

He designed fish, fish, fish of all kinds. Dolphins. Crabs. Shrimp. Lobsters. Eels. Anemones. Coral. Sea urchins. Sponges and jellyfish. On and on His miracles go! Let me ask you this—do you think God had fun thinking up an octopus with suction cups running up and down its tentacles and a sac full of ink? How bizarre and of course He did! Don't we all love to make fun things?

Genesis 1: 20-22
Job 39:26-27

When God looked into the beautiful blue sky, He must have thought how interesting it would be to have animals that could move through the air, high flying and free! There are thousands of different birds on the earth today—beautiful to look at and so many sounds and songs! They make nests of twigs, nests of mud, woven nests, nests in trees, and nests on the ground. Birds pollinate plants, eat insects and scatter seeds—an all around great plan! How do they navigate? By the stars? Some birds hunt and travel by night. By the angle of the sun? Some birds travel during the day. How do they find their nests in a forest of trees that all look alike? How do they migrate thousands of miles and find their way back home again? Are they guided by the earth's magnetic field?

No one knows for sure. That is God's secret between the birds and Himself.

When God had finished with the fish and birds He liked what He had done, and so God blessed them and told them to have lots of babies.

And that was the fifth day.

And now God wanted to put living things
on the dry parts of the earth.

So God began filling the earth with animals that roam and walk and run on land.
God was full of ideas and seems to have done some interesting experiments!
Some animals He created very early are still around, like turtles and tortoises and crocodiles.

And yet some animals He created were allowed to become extinct, like huge flying lizards
and all those dinosaurs that are so much fun to learn about!

Now most animals live all of their lives as wild things, for that is how God intended for those animals to be. Warthogs just do warthog things. Anteaters just do anteater things.

But some animals were put on the earth for special purposes—to help and serve what would be God's most miraculous creation. (Can you guess what that is? You ARE one!)

And so at last, when everything was in place and the time was right, God made a human being.
He made a man, and his name was Adam.
He was made in God's image, and God breathed life into him.
And then, to give the man a companion, a friend, a helper, and a mother for his children,
God made the man a wife and her name was Eve, "the mother of all the living".
And that was the sixth day.

Genesis 1: 26, 27
Genesis 3:20

God had prepared the earth perfectly for them, as we prepare for a wonderful party.
He gave them food, He gave them each other, He gave them the beauty of the day and night,
and all the animals He had put in the sea, the sky, and on the land.
God blessed them and told them that this beautiful Garden of Eden was their home,
and it was His wish that they would fill the earth with their children,
and grandchildren, and great-grandchildren and enjoy a wonderful life.

Genesis 1:28-31

The heavens and earth were finished! God was pleased and thought everything was very good!
And that was the sixth day.

Genesis 2: 1-3

Now God thought a rest time would be a good time,
so on the seventh day He rested,
and made that a holy day and a day of rest for all of us.

SCHOOL of the ARTS

So here
we all are.

When God
made people,
God created special beings
who can think and plan,
who can choose how they want to live and
to act, who can farm and invent things and
build things and make music and art, who can be
caretakers of the earth and of their families and
of other people, and who can use language so they can
talk to each other and to God Himself in their prayers.

God has known you and loved you since before you were born.
You are just as special to Him as a king or a queen or a president
or any other important person you can think of.
How great to know God loves everyone the same!
But there are certain ways that God hopes you will act
and think and feel about our world and others.

When God made people He decided that every person born would have
a special part of their being that would never die, just as God will never die.
That is our soul. And since that special part belongs to God when we
fill it with God and the things of God we have much joy!

We can ignore God. He gives us that choice. He did not want us to be robots that
He pushes around with a remote control. But do you suppose God ever
gives our hearts a little tug to tell us He is lonesome for us?

Genesis 9:13
Job 12:10
Jeremiah 33: 3
John 6:44
Revelation 3:20

These are the most important things God asks you to do:

To love Him with all your heart and to treat others
as you wish to be treated,
with kindness and love and good manners.

Everyone fails at this sometimes, but try and do your best.
It will make you feel good about yourself
and it makes the world so much nicer for everyone!

Matthew 22: 35-40
Luke 10:27

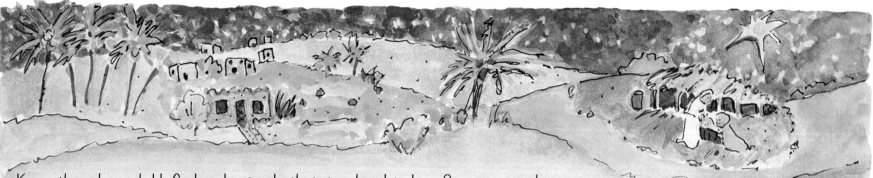

Know this, dear child: God understands that it is hard to love Someone you have never seen.

Deuteronomy 6:5
Jeremiah 29:13
Matthew 7: 7
John 6:40

But if you look for God, He will find you. That is His promise.
As you offer Him your prayers love will grow and grow.
Your little beginner prayers are just as fine to Him as the long, fancy prayers
of the most important grown-ups in church.

These four things are good to remember in your prayers:
1. Tell God He is wonderful, praise Him for His beautiful works, and tell Him you love Him.
    Whatever you do, do to His glory!!! That is worshipping God.
2. Ask God to forgive you if you have done some bad things you are sorry for doing or saying.
    Everyone does and says things they need to confess to God and ask for His forgiveness.
    And when we do, if we really mean it, God forgets we ever did that thing we are sorry for!
3. Thank God for the good things–the blessings–in your life.
4. Talk to God about problems you have, and ask His help. Pray for others.

There is so much more to God's story!
We will talk and learn more later.
May our good and beloved Lord bless and keep you.

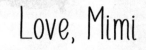

Love, Mimi

Lightning Source UK Ltd.
Milton Keynes UK
UKRC010248080921
389970UK00001BA/7

9 781977 240552